SCHEME

FOR

RENDERING PSALMODY

CONGREGATIONAL.

Price 2s. 6d.

SCHEME

FOR

RENDERING PSALMODY CONGREGATIONAL;

COMPRISING

A KEY TO THE SOL-FA NOTATION OF MUSIC,

AND

DIRECTIONS FOR INSTRUCTING A SCHOOL.

Second Edition, Enlarged.

THIS EDITION CORRESPONDS WITH THE THIRD EDITION OF THE SOL-FA TUNE BOOK.

NORWICH:
JARROLD AND SONS, 3, LONDON STREET.
LONDON:
HAMILTON, ADAMS, AND CO. 33, PATERNOSTER ROW.
M DCCC XXXIX.

CONTENTS.

PAGE.

OUTLINE of the Scheme with Prefatory Remarks 5

PART I.

Apology for a new Notation 16
Key to the Sol-fa Notation of Music 21
Observations on the same 39

PART II.

Directions for instructing a School, in Melody—Harmony—Rhythm 43
Tone 71
Expression 74

APPENDIX.

Directions for teaching the system of Notation by points, to a class of scholars already acquainted with the Sol-fa Notation, and rules for transferring a tune from the Old into the New Characters 81

OUTLINE OF THE SCHEME, &c.

The low state of psalmody in most of the churches belonging to the Establishment, is I believe, a fact generally acknowledged and frequently lamented. It is observed in the Life of Bishop Porteus, page 108. "Of all the services of our church none appear to me to have sunk to so low an ebb, or so evidently to need reform, as our parochial psalmody."

No effectual remedy, I conceive, can be suggested, unless the state of vocal music itself be materially improved. Amongst the superior orders of the community in this country, singing is at present very rarely cultivated at all by gentlemen; and few ladies have such an acquaintance with intervals, as to venture to sing the simplest psalm tune, unprompted or unsupported by an instrument, or by some voice better skilled than their own in sustaining an air in tune. Psalmody is therefore usually abandoned to the care of the illiterate, some of whom derive aid from a degenerate species of *sol-fa-ing,* still extant amongst them, and most of whom are accustomed in their youth, to strengthen their vocal organs in various ways which would be deemed unseemly in nurseries and academies for the children of gentlefolk. No wonder then, if psalmody has fallen into undeserved disrepute! Yet let it be remembered, Handel has not disdained to employ his genius on an art which appears to have been found serviceable as a handmaid to devotion by the most exalted characters mentioned in the Old and New Testament; and which has been sanctioned, there is reason to think, by the example of our Divine Master Himself. Shall we not then be willing to bestow some time and labour upon rescuing sacred song from its present degraded condition?

Let singing become a branch of national education, not only in schools for the children of labourers and mechanics, but in academies for young ladies and gentlemen, and the main point will be attained towards rendering psalmody truly congregational. A very little practice *well directed,* would soon produce a sufficient degree of skill, to render this employment highly attractive to the pupils; while it would afford healthful recreation in the midst of sedentary pursuits: independent of this advantage, when it is considered to what sacred purpose vocal skill may be applied, it cannot surely be justly deemed unworthy the attention of the highest class of society.

Two things are requisite before singing can become thoroughly congregational on *all* occasions.

First, there must be *a general acquaintance with notes,* unless none but hacknied tunes are to be performed.

Secondly, *not only melody but harmony* must be practised; otherwise many good voices, male and female, are necessarily silent, because the upper part is not within their compass.

A new "NOTATION OF MUSIC" has been contrived to facilitate the acquisition of musical science. Besides answering this purpose with the unlearned, it may prove useful to the scientific, when combined with the usual notation by points, in promoting the practice of *sol-fa-ing,* so favorable to the production of accuracy in tune, and so convenient to the practitioner who desires to avoid attaching sacred words to an air till all mechanical difficulty is surmounted.

The "DIRECTIONS FOR INSTRUCTING A SCHOOL" in Melody, Harmony, Rhythm, Tone and Expression, are designed to be serviceable in academies of young ladies and gentlemen. When applied to charity schools, the instructer can exercise discretion in omitting refinements, deemed unnecessary for the labouring classes of society.

A volume of "German Canons (or Singing Exercises) and Psalm Tunes" in which the letters of the *sol-fa* notation are placed under the points of the usual notation, has been prepared to aid the student (already possessed of musical science,) in comprehending the new system. The title of it is "Guide to Sol-fa-ing." The same canons and tunes expressed simply in the *sol-fa* notation are printed for the use of pupils in general.

The "German Canons" serve the purpose of a set of progressive lessons for teaching intervals, if sung merely in unison; but, when performed in parts, exercise the pupils likewise in harmony. The "Psalm Tunes" are arranged in two parts, being better adapted for the cultivation of harmony in schools for children, than when divided into treble, tenor and bass. Such an arrangement is also more calculated to promote *congregational* singing. If it be objected, how is a due proportion of voices for each part to be secured, if every member be at liberty to take first or second? I would answer, surely some orchestral effect might well be sacrificed to the devotional sympathy excited by the consciousness of union in the effort to sing praises: but this *due proportion* is, I believe, of much less consequence to the critical ear than is apprehended before experience.

One voice, singing a second, may be distinctly heard, though fifty voices perform in unison the upper part, and *vice versa;* and as acute sounds penetrate more easily than grave, there would be little danger of overpowering the melody of the upper part, even should a large majority of seconds ever be found in a congregation. It may also be observed that these seconds are so constructed as to contain nearly as much melody as the upper parts; therefore, if the original air were drowned (an effect not to be desired, it must be confessed) the predominant sounds might nevertheless be melodious.

If psalm tunes, arranged in the manner already described, were introduced into a church provided with an organ, it would be necessary for the organist to avoid any harmonies which would interfere with those adopted in these duets. In venturing this remark, I shelter myself under the authority of C. I. La Trobe, who observes in his preface (page vi.) to the "Hymn Tunes sung in the Church of the United Brethren," "There are generally some in the congregation that sing a kind of second or base to the tunes. The organist should also pay attention to these singers, and to avoid a discord, not play

Treble b c d e} when the congrega- {b c d e
Bass e a g f e} tion is used to sing {e a g e

or in the like instances. If he even justly prefer a bass, different from that marked in the tune book, yet he should sacrifice his opinion to the prevailing custom, if not entirely false; and even then be cautious and gentle in leading into the right track." I would here take the liberty of observing that I suspect an erroneous notion often prevails respecting the powers of the organ, tending to hinder the cultivation of congregational singing. Is it not frequently regarded as an instrument calculated to teach, or at least to lead psalmody? The inability of the organ, generally speaking, to express the *accent* in musical feet, renders it, in my opinion, a bewildering guide to novices, when it attempts to lead them; and it seems to me, to be too unwieldy an instrument to serve well as an accompaniment to an unskilful choir. I freely acknowledge its utility in prompting the pitch and air of a tune when played before the psalm is sung, and its power of drowning bad voices while the psalm is being sung; but, does not this latter quality tend to conceal the articulation of words, and to encourage indolence with respect to the cultivation of the human voice? I wish, however, to state, that I regard the organ a noble instrument in itself, the best substitute perhaps for human voices ever invented, capable also of heightening greatly the effect and beauty of vocal music, if used occasionally and judiciously in conjunction with a scientific choir. Whether a church be provided or unprovided with an organ, one good leader seems to me to be necessary, and two desirable. In places of worship where there are no gratuitous singers willing to undertake this office, a handbill might be circulated of the following description:—

Wanted.—Two voices, a high tenor and bass to lead the Psalmody in and to practise one hour with the congregation, weekly. No tunes or words to be sung, but those appointed by the minister. It is needless for any person to apply who cannot produce a respectable reference for character.

I will here suggest that the hour of practice alluded to in the above advertisement, might be devoted to a school (already established,) and liberty given to members of the congregation to attend. If a minister found it inconvenient to give his personal attention to this subject, he might probably procure as his deputy some musical member of his congregation, who would act under his sanction. Were "a whole assembly" able to read notes with facility, and furnished with printed tunes in conjunction with the words, how delightfully might be sung "with one consent," any psalm or hymn which suited the occasion! Such a change in the state of society cannot be effected rapidly in this country, where the mass of the population is notoriously deficient in musical science; but I think I may assert from experience acquired in a school consisting of more than sixty poor children, that vocal powers are very generally attainable, and the art of singing at sight from the *sol-fa* notation easy. If those who are already in possession of some musical science, would take the trouble of understanding this notation sufficiently for the purpose of instructing schools, if they would furnish themselves with the tunes designed to be used in the congregation, if they would cultivate their own voices as independent instruments and encourage others by their example to join in this part of public worship, the state of psalmody might, I am persuaded, soon be materially improved and in due time reformed. This object would also be materially promoted by a weekly association of the members of one or more congregations for the practice of psalmody, which might be effected with very little expense of time, if combined with some meeting for benevolent purposes, as the punctual and musical might exercise their voices till the majority were assembled. Parents who wish to cultivate the earliest vocal powers in their children, would find great advantage from admitting into their families a young nursery-maid, acquainted with the *sol-fa* notation, and the use of the Harmonicon which has been constructed to accord with this system. It will be seen by the above statement that I do not conceive good psalmody to be generally attainable without labour; but it is "*le premier pas qui coute,*" and many collateral advantages might result from the means employed, in the attainment of the end chiefly proposed.

For example, let the influence be considered of the cultivation of music *en masse* in a school of children: the precision requisite in this art renders *labour and discipline* necessary; both these have a good moral tendency and come practically recommended to the young community by pleasing associations. Health is also promoted by the exercise of the lungs, and the recreation afforded by so refreshing a variety in their occupations: music attracts them to the school, unites them in heart with their leader and with each other, composes while it raises the spirits, refines the mind and under judicious regulations, is calculated to favour piety.

PART I.

APOLOGY FOR THE SOL-FA NOTATION.

THE usual notation of music by points presents, if I mistake not, an unnecessary obstacle to the general cultivation of music, nor am I alone in my dissatisfaction; in the Quarterly Musical Magazine, 6th vol. page 473, for the year 1824, it is observed, "Any one who sets himself seriously to consider the present complex system of musical notation, easy as it may appear to those who have gradually mastered its difficulties, must, independent of all historical information, be convinced its basis was laid in the infancy of musical science, at a period when the attainments of musicians bore no proportion to those of the professors of the present day. So many characters have been from time to time added to keep pace with the improvements of different ages, that Guido himself, where he now to arise from his grave, would not recognize what is usually set down as his handy work." "The world will not much longer agree to be trammelled with the arbitrary characters of a barbarous age, bearing no analogy with the things which they are employed to represent." Whether the learned part of the musical world will or will not be thus discontented, I hope the above quotation will be received as an apology for the following attempt to relieve the majority of a congregation, from the "arbitrary characters" which deter them from science, at the very threshold of the art of music.

Four principal defects appear to me to exist in the notation by points, according to the usual mode of treating it. I will endeavour to state them.

1*st.*—*The inadequate representation of the scale on the staff,* no difference being made between the whole and half tones.

2*nd.*—*The encumbrance of non-accidental sharps and flats* which embarrass the practice and perplex the theory of music, rendering some keys much more abstruse than others, though the construction of all of them is equally simple.

3rd.—*The confusion arising from the contrivance of clefs,* by which device, characters varying in appearance, are used to express identical names and sounds.

4th.—*The needless variety and (in some instances) complexity of characters* employed to represent notes, differing in nothing except the octave where they occur. For example—observe the entire absence of analogy in the representation of five out of the six C's on the piano-forte.

I hope that the *sol-fa* notation not only provides a remedy for these defects, but adds the following advantages. It defines *Rhythm* more clearly, it characterises each *Interval* of the key, marks the *Scale,* expresses the relationship (generally) existing between keys where *Modulation* occurs, renders *Transposition* perfectly easy, and furnishes a set of syllables favorable to good *Intonation.*

The tendency of these improvements is, I think, to lead the pupil to sing better in tune, sooner at sight, and to imbibe more correct notions of the theory of music.

A convenient circumstance attending the *sol-fa* notation, is that it admits of being printed in common type.

The principal objection I anticipate to the use of the *sol-fa* notation, is, that the quantity of music already published in the usual notation by points, will be unintelligible to the student acquainted only with the new; this cannot be denied; and the practitioner would be circumstanced much like a person versed in the Greek language, while ignorant of the ancient character in which it is usually expressed. The new notation however; may easily and usefully be applied as an introduction to the pointed notation; and, in such a manner as to divest it of much of its seeming irrationality. (See Appendix.) I am persuaded that, on the whole, a more rapid progress would be made by pupils thus instructed, than by those who are obliged to encounter the defects, seeming and real, of the pointed notation at the commencement of their musical studies; while those who require no more knowledge than would qualify them for skill in psalmody, might easily be supplied with a collection of tunes printed in the *sol-fa* notation, ample enough for all the purposes of social and congregational worship.

TABLE OF TUNE.

	Pitch-Notes.	X	P	Z	U	J	W	O	Y	Q	H	V	K	X	Pitch-Notes.	
							Scale-Notes.									
a	H́		Ń		B́	T́	Ḿ	Ĺ	Ŕ	Ś	D́	F́			H́	a
a♭	z	Ŕ	Ś	D́	F́			N		B́	T́	Ḿ	Ĺ	Ŕ	z	g♯
g	y		B́	T́	Ḿ	Ĺ	Ŕ	Ś	D́	F́					y	g
g♭	x	D́	F́			N		B	T́	Ḿ	Ĺ	Ŕ	S	D́	x	f♯
f	w	T́	Ḿ	Ĺ	Ŕ	S	D́	F			B			T́	w	f or e♯
e	v			N		B	T́	M	Ĺ	Ŕ	S	D́	F		v	e
e♭	u	Ĺ	Ŕ	S	D́	F			N		B	T́	M	Ĺ	u	d♯
d	q	N		B	T́	M	Ĺ	R	S	D́	F			N	q	d or cx
d♭	p	S	D́	F			N		B	T́	M	Ĺ	R	S	p	c♯
c	o	B	T́	M	Ĺ	R	S	D	F			N		B	o	c or b
b or c♭	k	F			N		B	T	M	Ĺ	R	S	D	F	k	b
b♭	j	M	Ĺ	R	S	D	F			N		B	T	M	j	a♯
a	h		N		B	T	M	L	R	S	D	F			h	a
A♭	Z	R	S	D	F			Ǹ		B	T	M	L	R	Z	G♯
G	Y		B	T	M	L	R	S̀	D	F			Ǹ		Y	G
G♭	X	D	F			Ǹ		B̀	T	M	L	R	S̀	D	X	F♯
F	W	T	M	L	R	S̀	D	F̀			Ǹ		B̀	T	W	F or E♯
E	V			Ǹ		B̀	T	M̀	L	R	S̀	D	F̀		V	E
E♭	U	L	R	S̀	D	F̀			Ǹ		B̀	T	M̀	L	U	D♯
D	Q	Ǹ		B̀	T	M̀	L	R̀	S̀	D	F̀			Ǹ	Q	D or Cx
D♭	P	S̀	D	F̀			Ǹ		B̀	T	M	L	R̀	S̀	P	C♯
C	O	B̀	T	M̀	L	R̀	S̀	D̀	F̀			Ǹ		B̀	O	C or B♯
B or C♭	K	F̀			Ǹ		B̀	T̀	M̀	L	R̀	S̀	D̀	F̀	K	B
B♭	J	M̀	L	R̀	S̀	D̀	F̀			Ǹ		B̀	T̀	M̀	J	A♯
A	H		Ǹ		B̀	T̀	M̀	L̀	R̀	S̀	D̀	F̀			H	A
		G♭	D♭	A♭	E♭	B♭	F	C	G	D	A	E	B	F♯		

KEY

TO THE

SOL-FA NOTATION OF MUSIC.

TUNE.

TUNE is signified by Letters called Notes. Notes are of two kinds; Pitch-Notes and Scale-Notes. These are exemplified in the Table of Tune.

PITCH-NOTES.

(OR THE ARTIFICIAL CHROMATIC SERIES.)

The names of the Pitch-Notes are twelve in number, H J K O P Q U V W X Y Z. Each of them is considered a half tone above the preceding tone.

Two series of Pitch-Notes, one in capitals, the other in small letters, and an additional H correspond with the glasses in the *sol-fa*

Harmonicon, and with the usual compass of a cultivated child's voice. The upper series is expressed in small letters. The middle h agrees with the sound of the A on the second space in the treble staff of the usual notation by points.

SCALE-NOTES.

(OR THE NATURAL DIATONIC SERIES.)

Scale-Notes represent the tones and half tones which compose a scale or key. See the twelve columns of Scale-Notes arranged between two columns of Pitch-Notes in the Table of Tune.*

The names of the seven Scale-Notes, expressed by Roman letters, are (according to English pronunciation)

Doh, Ra, Me, Fah, Soh, Lah, Te.

These syllables are signified by their initials. The two Letters in Italics are called *Bah* and *Ne*.

* What may appear at first sight a thirteenth column, will be seen on examination to be merely a duplicate of the column headed by the Pitch-Note X.

Scale-Notes of the same name in the same column, having an acute sign (′) over them represent sounds an octave (viz. an 8th) higher than simple letters; those with a grave sign (‵) over them, represent sounds an octave lower. Each column contains two scales, the *Doh* scale and the *Lah* scale.

DOH SCALE.

The *Doh* scale is composed of the Roman letters exclusively. *Doh* is called the key-note, and its sound depends upon the Pitch-Note, which stands on a level with it in the table of tune. The key-note regulates the remaining six sounds, which bear the following relation to it.

T́ half a tone below D́
Ĺ whole tone and half below D́
S three whole tones and half above D
F two whole tones and half above D
M two whole tones above D
R whole tone above D
D key-note.

LAH SCALE.

In ***descending,*** all the notes expressed by the Roman letters are used, but in ***ascending, Fah*** and ***Sole*** are omitted, and two notes half a tone higher are inserted, ***Bah*** and ***Ne.***

Lah is called the key-note, its sound depends upon the Pitch-Note, the fourth letter below the one corresponding with its relative ***Doh.*** Thus, if ***Doh*** stands on a level with O, its relative ***Lah*** will be on a level with H.

ROW OF TUNE.

The sounds in the columns of the Table of Tune, are expressed in the following manner in rows.

D̀ R̀ M̀ F̀ S̀ L, T D R M F S Ĺ, T́ D́

The above row exhibits a regular succession of ascending notes in the ***Doh*** scale through two octaves. The following a regular succession of descending Scale-Notes.

D T L S F M R D T L S F M R D

A Pitch-Note is placed at the beginning of a row, to signify the pitch of the first Scale-Note in it. (See ***Wakefield,*** Sol-fa Tune Book.)

The Pitch-Note of the column (or columns) in which the tune is performed, is placed at the head of it.

MODULATION.

Modulation is the art of passing from one scale to the other, or from one column to another, in the Table of Tune.

Vocal music seldom overpasses the boundaries of three contiguous columns. These contain what are usually termed the six related keys; three in the *Doh* scale, and three in the *Lah* scale. The three in the *Doh* scale are expressed in the musical ladder; the intervals which characterize the *Lah* scale are omitted for the sake of simplicity with beginners; but the *Bah* and *Ne* which mark them, may be inserted afterwards, in red ink, when the pupil is sufficiently advanced to practise the *Lah* scale.

The mode of expressing Modulation is, I trust, improved, since the publication of the "Guide to Sol-fa-ing." The discrepance which now exists between the "Guide," and the third edition of the "Sol-fa Tune Book," does not (with slight exceptions) concern the *ear*, but only the *eye;* therefore different performers may sing from the two books at the same time without inconvenience.

SECTION OF A MUSICAL LADDER.

s	D	f
	T	m
f		
m	L	r
r	S	d
		t
d	F	
t	M	l
l	R	s
s	D	f
	T	m
f		
m	L	r

When the singer passes from one column into another, a certain letter (or letters) is added to the initial of the syllable of the first note in the new column, to signify to the *ear* its distance from the preceding column. For example, in making one move to the left of the original column, suppose the first note in the new column to be *sole,* substitute *i* for *ole,* and call the new note *si* instead of *sole.*

TABLE OF MODULATION.

	To the left.	To the right.	
One column	*i*	u	frequently used.
Two columns	*aw*	oo	seldom used.
Three columns	*aze*......	oze	

Modulation, which proceeds three columns to the right or left, exceeds the bounds of the Ladder, and does not occur in the tunes already printed.

Modulation still more remote may be expressed by Chromatic Intervals, which will be explained hereafter.

The change of column is further marked to the *eye,* by the form of the letters which correspond with those in the Musical Ladder.

EXAMPLES OF MODULATION.

N. B. The first letter in the new column is the nearest of its name to the last note sung in the preceding column.

In *Abridge* there is a change from the middle column to that on the right. S tu

In *Brunswick,* from the middle column to the left. S *si*

In the 149*th Psalm* there is no change of column, but a change from the *Doh* to the *Lah* scale. S N

In the 96*th Psalm* there is a change of column from the right to the left hand column. m *baw*

In the 148*th Psalm* from the left to the right hand column. *l* moo

CHROMATIC INTERVALS.

A Chromatic Interval is a sound which occurs between any of the whole tones of the Diatonic Series. The diphthong *oy,* added to the initial of a *sol-fa* syllable, elevates it half a tone; *ow* depresses it half a tone. No use has been made of these intervals in the "Guide to Sol-fa-ing," nor in the third edition of the Sol-fa Tune Book.

ORNAMENTAL NOTES.

Ornamental Notes, which may be expressed or omitted at discretion, are printed half the size of the other letters.

CORRESPONDENCE BETWEEN THE SOL-FA NOTATION OF MUSIC AND THE OPEN SOL-FA HARMONICON.

In the front part of the *sol-fa* Harmonicon is a row of twenty-five glasses, which, when struck with a hammer adapted to the instrument, emit sounds answering to the Pitch-Notes in the Table of Tune.

Behind these glasses is an elevated rotary cylinder. On this cylinder are drawn twelve horizontal lines, on which are expressed the Scale-Notes which are arranged in twelve columns in the Table of Tune. This cylinder is enclosed, with the exception of a long horizontal aperture, for the purpose of exhibiting whichever line of scale-notes is to serve as an index to the glasses.

If there be modulation in the psalm tune to be performed, the aperture may be increased, so as to uncover the two or three scales which may be required.

TABLE OF RHYTHM.

<table>
<tr><th></th><th colspan="8">Number of feet contained in each line.</th><th>Nature of the Musical feet to be adapted to a line of poetry.</th></tr>
<tr><th></th><th>1st</th><th>2nd</th><th>3rd</th><th>4th</th><th>5th</th><th>6th</th><th>7th</th><th>8th</th><th></th></tr>
<tr><td>Common Metre.....</td><td>4</td><td>3</td><td>4</td><td>3</td><td></td><td></td><td></td><td></td><td>. | or .(| .)</td></tr>
<tr><td>Long Metre.........</td><td>4</td><td>4</td><td>4</td><td>4</td><td></td><td></td><td></td><td></td><td>. | or .(| .)</td></tr>
<tr><td>Short Metre.........</td><td>3</td><td>3</td><td>4</td><td>3</td><td></td><td></td><td></td><td></td><td>. | or .(| .)</td></tr>
<tr><td>Proper 149th Psalm</td><td>4</td><td>4</td><td>4</td><td>4</td><td></td><td></td><td colspan="2">Chorus</td><td>. | .</td></tr>
<tr><td>Proper 96th Psalm</td><td>4</td><td>4</td><td>4</td><td>4</td><td>4</td><td>4</td><td>4</td><td>4</td><td>.(| .) except the chorus . |</td></tr>
<tr><td>Proper 148th Psalm</td><td>3</td><td>3</td><td>3</td><td>3</td><td>2</td><td>1</td><td>1</td><td>2 rept.</td><td>.(| .) except 6th and 7th lines *** . | .</td></tr>
<tr><td>Doncaster .. ..</td><td>4</td><td>3</td><td>4</td><td>3</td><td>4</td><td>3</td><td>4</td><td>3</td><td>. | except 5th line | .</td></tr>
<tr><td>Easter Hymn.......</td><td>4</td><td>4</td><td>4</td><td>4</td><td></td><td></td><td></td><td></td><td>| . ! . and | .(! .) besides two feet (sung to the word hallelujah) combined thus (| . !).(| .)(! .)</td></tr>
<tr><td>St. Columba.........</td><td>4</td><td>4</td><td>4</td><td>4</td><td>4</td><td>4</td><td>4</td><td>4</td><td>| . the last foot in 2nd, 4th, 6th, and 8th lines is composed of combined beats.</td></tr>
</table>

RHYTHM.

Rhythm consists principally in the due arrangement of *time* and *accent;* and is, I conceive, analogous to metre in poetry. The points of division of time are chiefly marked by bars and dots. A bar | represents a loud beat, a dot . a soft beat; the former should be struck on something more sonorous than the latter, and they should be repeated at regular intervals with the exactness of the clicking of a clock. A beat, when performed, accompanies the commencement of the note which immediately follows it on paper.

Every tune is composed of a certain number of lines, correspondent in general to the lines in a stanza of poetry; these lines consist of feet; the rhythm of a tune depends on the nature and number of these lines. A simple foot consists of one loud beat and of one or two soft beats. A compound foot consists of two loud and of two soft beats, or of two loud and four soft beats, or of three loud and of three soft beats; the predominant accent is expressed by a bar, an inferior accent by an interjection stop !

When a letter is ~~preceded by one of the same name, and connected with it~~ by a hyphen, it simply prolongs the sound of the ~~first~~ note. See *Wakefield*, second row, ~~B-.B~~

It has been observed, that tunes are composed of lines; lines, of feet; and feet, of beats. Occasionally beats require subdivision; when this is the case, a comma (or commas) is employed. See *Wakefield*, ~~M-,M R.D~~

When poetry is attached to the music, the note or notes which occupy the time of one beat, generally belong to one syllable; but if the notes of two or more beats are included in a parenthesis, they all belong to one syllable of the poetry. See *Wakefield*, (M- ,M R.D)

A star * over a *sol-fa* note signifies that a syllable of the words is to be attached to that alone, contrary to the usual adaptation of the musical to the poetical feet in the same tune. See *Brunswick*, D̊.M̊

The Table of Rhythm is to be read as follows:—

When the Rhythm accords with Common Metre, (no repetition of words or other variations occurring,) the first line contains 4 feet, the second line 3 feet, the third line 4 feet, the fourth line 3 feet. Each foot consists of one soft and of one loud beat adapted (when there is no irregularity in the poetry) to one unaccented and to one accented syllable; or the foot may consist of three beats, in which case, the first is adapted to the unaccented syllable and the two last to the accented syllable. (See page 32.)

At the head of each tune in the Sol-fa Tune Book, a specimen of the feet of which it is composed is given, and the time is marked of each beat, as designated by Maelzel's Metronome. Although a standard of time is suggested for each tune, yet some deviation from it will be desirable occasionally, on account of shades of difference in the character of words which may be attached to it. I, II, &c. is placed over or under a note which corresponds with the beginning of a line in a stanza. A pitch-note is situated opposite the commencement of every row of scale-notes, according with the first scale-note in it.

A figure between two beats is a rest, or time for silence. See examples of rests in the 11th canon.

½ signifies a rest, the duration of half the time from one beat to another.

¼ a rest, the duration of a quarter of the time from one beat to another.

The accented parts of a musical foot ought always to accord with the accented parts of a poetical foot, except when a poetical foot contains no accent. In the tune called *Brunswick* in Dr. Miller's selection of psalms, care has been taken to vary the tune to suit the different stanzas. For example in the first stanza, the tune begins thus—

.	* D .* M .F	S
	Lord hear the	voice

In the 7th,

.D (	M-.M) .F	S
And	when thy	bound &c.

If a choir is not sufficiently scientific to make these variations, it is desirable to choose a tune which will, without alteration, agree with the poetry in the first foot of the first stanza.

The following is an example of a tune in the *Sol-fa* notation.

MOUNT EPHRAIM. S. M. *Plaintive.*

Column Q. H. Foot .(| .) Metronome 60.

Q . D (M .R) .D (S- ,S F .M) .R
I
Q . D (D .T) .D (M- ,M R .D) .T

Q (D- .D) .D (T. L) .S (R- ,R D
II
Q (D- .D) .M (R .tu) .d (m- ,m r

p .T) .L (S- .S) .F (M- ,M R .D) .L
III
h .d) .t (d- .d) .m (Di- .D) .F

h (S- ,S F .M) .S (L- ,L S .L) .T
X (M- ,M R .D) .M (F- ,F M .F) .R

q (D- .D) .L (S F .M R) .D F M
IV
X (M- .M) .F (M R .D T) .D R D

V (.R- .R) (D- .D
P (.T- .T) (D- .D

OBSERVATIONS

ON THE

SOL-FA NOTATION.

The Pitch-Notes are a selection of letters not employed in the nomenclature of the old notation by points, nor yet in the *Sol-fa* letters of the new.

The syllable *Te* is substituted for the usual syllable *Se*, that the initial may be distinguished from that employed for *Sole*.

The grave and acute signs are disposed in such a manner, as to make *Lah* the lowest of the seven *Sol-fa* letters. The reason for this arrangement is, that it accords with the analogy discovered by Sir Isaac Newton to exist between the proportions of the prismatic colours and the divisions of a musical string in the ascending Minor Scale, the space from *Lah* to *Te* being the same as that occupied by violet, the space from *Te* to *Doh* by indigo, from *Doh* to *Ra* by blue, from *Ra* to *Me* by green, from *Me* to *Bah* by yellow, from *Bah* to *Ne* by orange, from *Ne* to the octave above *Lah* by red. (See Sir J. Hawkins, vol. v. page 67—69, for this fact; and for the precise divisions of a musical string, see a short "Introduction to the Theory of Harmonics," by J. Marsh, Esq. plate following page 8.) *Fah* and *Sole* are not to be found in the scale according with the prismatic colours; but may not the Major Scale, to which they more particularly belong, bear in some way that resemblance to an unbroken ray of light, which the Minor does to a broken ray? Not only on account of the analogy above mentioned, am I inclined to regard *Lah* as the lowest note of the diatonic scale, but I am confirmed in this view of the subject, by considering the terms applied by theoretical musicians to six of the seven intervals of which it is composed. (See Callcott's Musical Grammar, page 134.)

Lah is the *submediant,* viz. mediant *below* the Tonic.

Te the *subsemitone* or leading half tone *below* the Tonic.

Ra the *supertonic.*

Me the mediant, between the tonic and dominant, therefore *above* the former.

Sole is the dominant or fifth *above* the key-note.

Fah it must be confessed, is termed the *subdominant* or fifth below the key-note, yet it is said to be the tone below the dominant, (therefore the fourth above the tonic) in the regular scale of seven notes; does it not also bear the character of a sensible note leading downwards, as much as *Te* does that of a sensible note leading upwards? It may be worth remarking for curiosity's sake, that in the division of a musical string, *Fah* occupies the middle point between the tonic and its octave.

The *sol-fa* notation has been described as applicable only to the compass of the Harmonicon, but by doubling the series of pitch-notes above with the addition of acute accents, and by doubling the series below with the addition of grave accents, and by placing *two* grave accents over the letters expressive of the very lowest tones, more than the compass of the Piano-forte would be embraced.

PART II.

DIRECTIONS FOR

INSTRUCTING A SCHOOL.

APPARATUS.

The Apparatus required for the first process in organizing a choir, consists of

A "*Guide to Sol-fa-ing.*" Price 3s. (See page 9)

A dozen *Sol-fa Tune Books.* Price 3d. each. (See page 9.)

A *Musical Ladder,* in large type. Price 2d. (See page 27.)

A *Sol-fa Harmonicon.* (See page 31.)

Sol-fa Harmonicons are made by Mr. Reuben Warne, No. 3, Calvert Street, Norwich. The price of the open *Sol-fa* Harmonicon, which extends nominally from A below the treble staff, to A above the treble staff, including all the semitones, is £2. 10s. The price of the keyed *Sol-fa* Harmonicon, of similar compass, is £5.* The pitch of the Harmonicon is in fact an octave higher than the pitch of a child's voice; this circumstance is rather an advantage, if I mistake not, with respect to the cultivation of the ear for tune, on account of the greater nicety of intervals in proportion to their altitude. The height of the pitch tends also, in my opinion, to counteract the proneness in singers, to that common defect—FLATNESS.

This instrument is not absolutely necessary if the superintendent of the school be skilled in denoting the pitch of the key-note, but it is a useful appendage to the system in various ways. It is not indeed sufficiently powerful

* The cylinder of this instrument is on a smaller scale than that which is in the open Harmonicon, and is placed behind a slit in the upright board just above the keys.

to lead the voices of a school, still less of a congregation; but may be employed to prompt the pitch in either. The Harmonicon renders a school less dependent on any particular teacher than it might otherwise be; it aids a school-mistress materially in acquiring new tunes, it tends to promote the love of music, and therefore the cultivation of it amongst the superior scholars, if they are permitted to remain after school hours to practise upon it. The purity of its tone presents an excellent example to the voice, and its freedom from fluctuation in tune gives it a superiority, in this respect, to almost every other musical instrument, in assisting the vocal practitioner. The exercise of playing on the Harmonicon qualifies the pupils the better for pointing to the intervals on the Musical Ladder, and thus renders them the more capable of instructing their school-fellows, as will be seen hereafter; while familiarity with the arrangement of the intervals on the cylinder of the Harmonicon, improves their knowledge of the theory of music, and thus helps to prepare them for singing at sight, and for translating tunes from the notation by points into the *Sol-fa* notation.

A *Piano-forte Card* is serviceable in illustrating the system to a piano-forte player, who is unprovided with a keyed *Sol-fa* Harmonicon. Price 1s.

A *Metronome* would be advantageous, but where this is regarded too expensive an instrument, a graduated pendulum may supply its place in a great measure. The superiority of the former to the latter consists in this;—the Metronome, if I mistake not, expresses the divisions of time in a more definite manner than the pendulum, and not only informs the eye but the ear; it is besides more convenient, not requiring the motion of the hand to keep up its vibrations, while the tune is being performed. The imperturbable calmness with which the Metronome clicks the time, to an enthusiastic pupil, who would convert by degrees an *andante* into an *allegro,* makes it answer the purpose of a master in an important requisite in the art of music.

LESSONS IN MELODY, HARMONY, RHYTHM.

"MELODY consists in a succession of single musical sounds, HARMONY in a combination of those sounds, according to the rules of composition." RHYTHM chiefly depends on the due arrangement of time and accent.

The instructress (a female's voice is perhaps more easily imitated by children than a man's,) will first teach them the names, *not the sounds*, of the seven *sol-fa* letters in the *Doh* mode,

viz. Doh, Rah, Me, Fah, Sole, Lah, Te, Doh,

at the same time pointing to the intervals on the Musical Ladder. When these can be read by the pupils upwards and downwards, they are prepared for the first singing lesson, which will consist, in—

I.

The ascending Melody of the common chord in the *Doh* mode in the column Q, viz. (D key with two sharps,) the common chord of the key-note in this column, being the best adapted to the compass of the majority of children's voices. She will tell the children to listen while she sings *Doh* and to imitate her voice, when she points to the note on the Musical Ladder, her pattern sound should be soft, but she will do well to join the school with several loud repetitions of it, resembling the tolling of a bell. If this exercise be tolerably performed, pursue the same plan with *Me*, then with *Sole*, then with the upper *Doh*. If the children have been much unaccustomed to singing, they will at first perhaps not be able to reach more than *Doh, Me, Sole*, if so, the upper *Doh* must be omitted for a time.

II.

When the timidity and merriment, usual at these first efforts, have subsided, let the teacher sing *Doh* or *Me* with each child individually; let those children who err unconsciously and materially, be put together and told not to join for the present, or very softly; thus situated, they are less likely to mislead the rest, and the other children are rendered careful. After this investigation, the exercise of the common chord may again be repeated by all simultaneously, when the performance of it will probably be found much improved.

III.

Select about a dozen of the cleverest children and prepare them as leaders to the rest of the school. When this class is able to sing firmly without the aid of their preceptress, *Doh,* D, D, D, *Me,* M, M, M, *Sole, &c.* *Ḋoh, &c.* the teacher may gradually introduce them to the *Harmony* of the common chord, by softly sustaining with the syllable *ah,* the key-note during the last three *Me's,* the third of the key in the same manner, while the pupils sing the last three upper *Ḋohs ;* thus—

She may also sing in the same way the third above *Doh,* viz. *Me,* and the third above *Me,* viz. *Sole.*

IV.

The Preceptress may next direct the pupils to sing *Doh* over and over again till told to stop; as soon as they have sung four *Dohs* she will accompany them with repetitions of *Me.* She may then divide the class into two parts, let one half of the pupils sing *Dohs* repeatedly as before, and the other half (as soon as the first four *Dohs* have been executed) join the Teacher in singing *Me, Me,* &c. when they are firm so far, the Teacher may add as a third part *Sole, &c.* and afterwards divide the pupils into three companies, and then into four, till at last the exercise may be thus performed, the Teacher approaching each company in turn, joining them in their respective note and thus giving a signal for taking fresh breath.

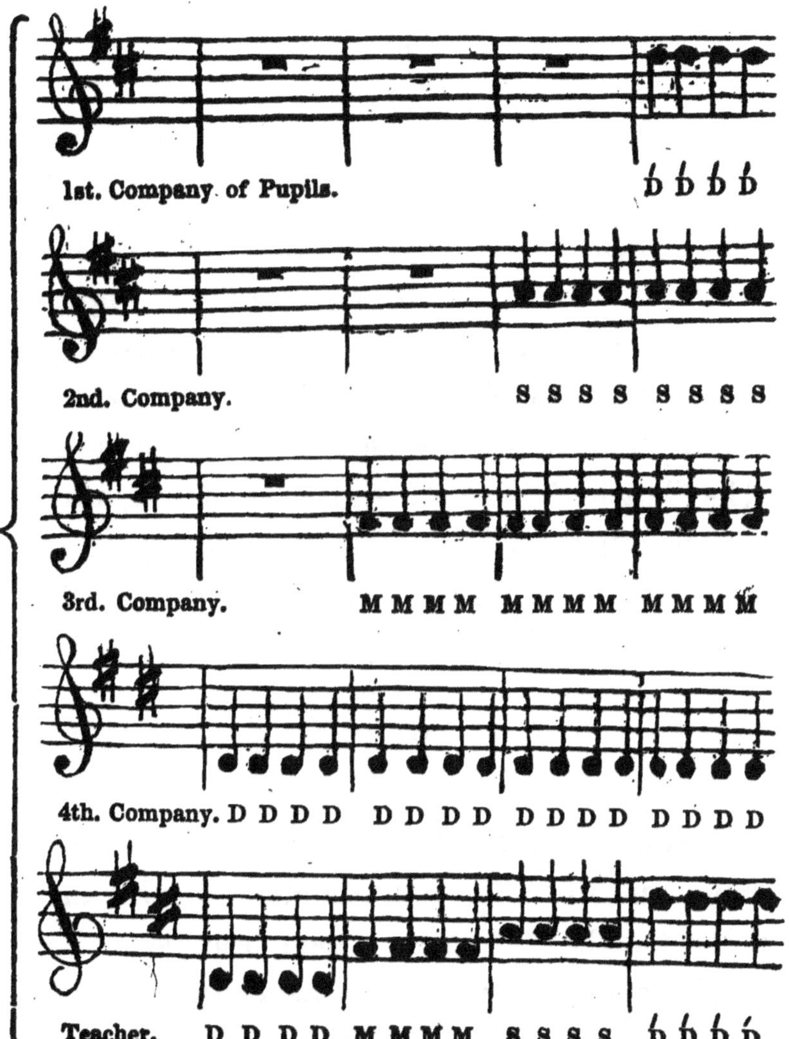

The Teacher will also beat time, marking the Rhythm, (See page 33.) The different companies should change parts till each is perfect in all.

V.

The above exercise may then be varied by substituting a semibreve for each measure* of four crotchets, the pupils should then be directed to imitate the *steady tone* of an organ, (See Lesson xviii. on Tone.) In the course of the exercise, the Teacher may sing an *arpeggio* accompaniment on the chord of the key-note. The Teacher's line of sixteen crotchets may also be converted into a Canon in four parts as soon as some leaders have been taught to beat time.

VI.

Beating time in different measures may be taught in the following manner. Strike the palms together to express a loud beat, bend the hands into fists and strike them together for a soft beat. Let the Teacher say | *loud, soft* | *loud, soft, &c.;* then count | 1 .2 | 1 .2, &c. striking palms and fists alternately, the children

* By a measure is here meant all the notes contained between two bars, viz. two perpendicular lines.

imitating the action of her hands. She would in so doing have marked the musical feet, of which the first and second canons are composed. See *Sol-fa Tune Book,* third edition, foot | . The feet of the third canon, each of which consists of a bar and two dots, | . . she would express in words as follows. *Loud, soft, soft, Loud, soft, soft;* and *One, two, three, One, two, three,* &c. The feet of the fourth* canon ! . | . thus—Soft, soft, loud, soft, Soft, soft, loud, soft, and Three, four, one, two, Three, four, one, two, &c. After counting some measures, the Teacher might sing what she next intends to teach the children, while the beating continues. The beating of the time of rests may be taught by striking the fore-fingers downwards at the loud or accented, and sideways at the soft or unaccented part of the measures. When rests intervene during singing, the Teacher should speak the figures indicative of the number of rests which precede the next note; these figures bear no relation to the part of the measure in which they occur. See for

* Although four beats form a compound foot, yet, for simplicity's sake, I should avoid mentioning the semi-loud beat to young beginners.

example, the eleventh canon in the *Guide to Sol-fa-ing;* or, in the *Sol-fa Tune Book,* third edition.

The intended leaders of the canons should not only be taught to beat time with their hands, but with a pointer or ruler, as one hand will sometimes be engaged in holding a book. The loud beats must be expressed by a stroke on something sonorous, the soft beats may be struck on the book.

VII.

The instructress may then teach them the first of the German Canons, pointing to the notes on the Musical Ladder, she will herself dictate alone half of it, and then require the class to imitate and join her in the repetition of it; the same with the latter half. The second, third, fourth, and fifth canons may be taught in portions in a similar manner. When the pupils have accomplished these in unison, and when several of them are enabled to point to the intervals on the Ladder, they should be introduced to the same canons in the printed tune books. For this purpose, each child should be furnished with a book; the instructress will then dictate the first canon in portions; the class repeating each portion simultaneously. (The line between designates the portion dictated at once.)

1st Canon.—Column Q—Foot, loud beat soft beat—Number 60—Acute D́oh—Sole—Me—Doh—Doh—Me—Sole—Acute D́oh.

2nd Canon.—Column Q—Foot, loud beat, soft beat—Number 60—Doh—Doh—Sole—Sole—Acute D́oh—Rest, one beat—Me—Me—Me—Me—Doh—Rest, one beat.

After reading a canon, the whole class may sing it in unison, each child pointing to the note she sings; the pupils may then learn to sing the five earliest canons in parts. I would recommend that the fifth be taught first, the melody being more attractive than that of the preceding canons, and therefore more easily maintained against the other parts. While the pupils sing it in unison, the instructress may add a second part softly with the syllable *ah,* then louder with the *Sol-fa* syllables, afterwards she may divide the pupils into two companies, and after dictating the leading notes to the two companies in succession, sing a third part herself, and so on till all the four parts are distributed amongst four companies; one girl in each company should beat time with a pointer as soon as it is the turn for her company to begin.

VIII.

The twelve earliest canons include all the intervals of the *Doh* mode; when these are acquired, it would be well to exercise the pupils in singing the diatonic scale, regularly up and down, the instructress pointing to the Ladder, and occasionally accompanying the pupils by an addition of thirds and sixths above or below the notes they sing. If the exercise be performed very slowly, an *arpeggio* accompaniment on the various intervals of the scale may be added by the instructress.

IX.

The pupils should then be taught to *read* the *second* of a tune. The instructress dictates it in portions, each of which consists of as many notes as belong to a beat, (except when a note exceeds the length of a beat, in which case the portion must consist of two beats,) the leaders and pupils repeat each portion simultaneously pointing at the same time to the notes in their books. A simple tune containing no change of key, and only two beats in a measure, should first be taught; for example, the University. See *Sol-fa Tune Book*.

University.—Common Metre.—Column Q. —Foot, soft beat, loud beat.—Number 60.— Second part.—First line.—Me—Doh—Te Doh —Me—Ra Doh—Te—grave Sole—Doh.— Second line.—Me—Doh—Fah Me—Ra—Doh —grave Sole.—Third line.—Sole Fah—Me— Doh—Fah—Me—Doh—Te Doh—Ra—Fourth line.—Me—Fah—Me Ra—Doh—Te—Doh.

The varieties which occur in the following

tunes are to be read as follows;—but it is better to avoid perplexing the minds of the pupils with them before they have occasion to learn the tunes which contain them.

WAKEFIELD.

.(| .)—Foot, soft beat, loud beat, soft beat, combine the two last beats.

M- ,M R—Me, half-beat and a quarter, Ra.
D- .D—Doh, two beats.

BRODSWORTH.

If a note extends beyond the time of one beat, a child must read as many notes as belong to two beats.

D- .D ,R M—Doh, beat and half, Ra, Me.
.F ,M R—Fah, half-beat, Me, Ra.
M R—Small capital Me, Ra.

ABRIDGE.

tu-.t—tu right column, two beats.
SI—Si middle column.

BRUNSWICK.

* *
D .M—Doh, one syllable, Me, one syllable.
si —— si left column.

OLD 100.

½ M—Rest, Me.

96TH PSALM.

baw—baw, left column.

148TH PSALM.

moo—moo, right column.

DONCASTER.

R D—Ornamental Ra, Doh.

X.

When the second part of the tune has been read, the instructress sings it alone, while the pupils point to each note in their books, under the superintendence of some person who passes from one to another of the choir, to see if they do so correctly. The whole class then perform it; when they are able to sing without the aid of their instructress, she will insinuate the upper part with the syllable *ah,* increase the sound by degrees, and in due time add the *Sol-fa* syllables.

XI.

The pupils may then read the upper part in the same manner, and as soon as they sing it with firmness, the instructress should add the second with the syllable *ah,* &c. Half the class may subsequently sing the upper part while the other half sing the second, and *vice versa.* If the seconds are unsteady, let those who sing the upper part be placed at some distance from them, and directed not to begin till two or three notes have been sung by the seconds.

XII.

After two or three simple tunes have been thus taught, one with change of key may be acquired in the same manner; but before the pupils sing it from their books, it is desirable to practise them in it a little with their eye on the Musical Ladder, while the teacher points to the intervals, that they may clearly understand the meaning of a change of column. Several of the pupils should be exercised by turn, in pointing to the intervals on the Ladder.

The scholars should be well versed in the relative situation of the *Sol-fa* letters in the three columns of the Musical Ladder, and be questioned in the following manner, on the ascending scale.

What is to the right of DOH ? fah.
Of RA ? sole.
Of ME ? lah.
Of FAH ? a blank.

What is just above the blank ? te.

What is to the right of SOLE ? doh.
Of LAH ? ra.
Of TE ? me.

In descending the Ladder, let the scholar be questioned as to the situation of the *sol-fa* letters to the left of the middle column.

XIII.

When the select class can perform the harmony of the common chord in imitation of the tolling of a bell, and of the tones of an organ; when they can execute the twelve earliest canons in parts; when they can sing the *Doh* scale upwards and downwards, and both parts of two or three psalm tunes; when they can beat time with their hands and with pointers; and when several of them can point with facility to the intervals on the Musical Ladder—the class is prepared* for assisting the teacher in

* Such is the degree of preparation I would recommend, where it can be conveniently afforded; but if the time of an organizer be too limited to allow so much of it exclusively to the select class; and if the choir cannot be left under the superintendence of a person sufficiently effective to introduce the *Sol-fa* system into the mass of the school, the select class might be employed sooner in assisting their schoolfellows in learning what they themselves have acquired. Regular attendance in the pupils is so important to the success of the organizer, that I venture to suggest the expediency of offering a reward to every one who does not fail in attendance more than twice during a certain number of lessons.

organizing the whole school, which may then be taught the exercise described in lessons III and IV. In teaching the harmony of the common chord, let the mass of the scholars make one company, led by one of four divisions of the class of leaders. When the harmony of the common chord is accomplished, the leaders may sing a canon in unison while the pupils beat time with their hands. Portions of it may then be sung to the school by the teacher, and echoed simultaneously by the pupils, aided by the leaders; the leaders may be employed by turn in pointing to the Ladder during this exercise, while the remainder of this select band beat time with their pointers. The pupils in general should cease to beat time with their hands while singing, and should be directed to hold themselves in a quiet erect posture.

When five canons have been acquired in unison, the fifth may be put into parts, the mass of the school being led by one of four divisions of leaders, one of the pupils of which this division consists pointing to the intervals on the Ladder, another beating time. The preceding canons may afterwards be put into parts. In process of time the pupils may be equally divided, if furnished with a sufficient number of Ladders and books,* and placed under the superintendence of particular leaders. The lower classes may sing from Ladders, the higher from books. According to the number of parts of which the canon consists, let the instructress give the word of command, "four leaders;" "three leaders;" "two leaders;" "eight leaders;" at which word appointed leaders should elevate their pointers, as a proof that they know which are to act as leaders, and as a sign to the scholars to what company they individually belong; also as a direction to a general leader, who goes round to all the companies in turn to aid them in singing the leading notes of the canon.

* In the school alluded to, page 13, every child is required on being admitted into the school, to purchase a "Sol-fa Tune Book," unless she prefers relinquishing her claim to the half of a shilling ticket, to which she would be entitled at the end of the quarter, in case of regular attendance. The book is laid aside till she is capable of using it; and is kept at the school-room till she ceases to be a scholar, when she is permitted to carry it home.

XIV.

Before a tune is taught in which the *Lah* mode occurs, this scale may be introduced to the pupils by the following progressive exercises.

1st. D́ T́ Ĺ S F M R D

2nd. D́ T́ Ĺ S F M R D T L

3rd. Ĺ S F M R D T L

4th. L T D R M Ĺ S F M R D T L

5th. L T D R M N Ĺ S F M R D T L

6th. L T D R M B N Ĺ S F M R D T L

Point out that B N L answer to L T D in the scale three columns to the right, in the table of tune, or three rows below on the cylinder in the Harmonicon.

XV.

Care must be taken to prevent a tune from degenerating. As soon as it has been practised sufficiently to be known by heart, the indifferent singers are apt to become courageous, and the best careless, and the teacher discouraged by finding the adage reversed, "practice makes perfect." The principal defect will probably be flatness; and the flatness will chiefly occur at *Me* and *Te:* especially in the descending scale. This defect may be checked in several ways. 1st. Point out the error and remind the children of the half tones in the scale. 2ndly. Divide the tune into many short portions, set them a pattern of each portion before they sing it—observe those portions where they fail most and make them sing them a certain number of times before they proceed to other portions. 3rdly. Sacrifice the time and sing the tune slowly to a second, and do not leave a tone till it is in tune with the tone in the second part; (as it is supposed the instructress can hold the note longer than the generality of the pupils, it will end from this cause, if from no other, better in tune than it began.) On such an occasion the pupils must watch the lips of the instructress, or the movements of the pointer on the Musical Ladder, to know when they are to proceed to a new note. 4thly. Practise *Me* with the *Doh* below, and with the *Sole* above; *Te* with the *Sole* below; then with the *Ra* above. Another useful method of improving the upper part, is to make the whole school sing the second, while the instructress sings the upper part. But sometimes it may be expedient to lay aside a hacknied tune for a time, and when brought forward again, confine the majority of the choir to the second, till bad habits are in a measure lost.

As a preventive to general defectiveness in tune, it may be desirable frequently to precede the performance of an air by the exercises on the harmony of the common chord, in lesson IV. Sometimes it is sufficient for the teacher to sing the key note, and while she continues to sustain it, let her make a signal for the whole school to unite with her in singing it.

XVI.

It is desirable to give the leaders a distinct idea of the rules by which the words of a psalm are applied to the notes. Point out to them that when there is no parenthesis, one syllable is regularly attached to the note or notes sounded during the time of one beat. When there is a parenthesis, one syllable appertains to all the notes sounded during the time of the beats included in the parenthesis.

This class may easily learn to attach the words of a chant to the music, if the words be arranged* like the specimen of the hundredth psalm, mentioned in a note at the conclusion of the "Sol-fa Tune Book." The mass of the pupils may be taught to unite with them in this way:—let the teacher speak the words which belong to the chanting note; let them hear the class of leaders, (who it is supposed are furnished with copies of the above-mentioned chant,) add the words which belong to the *timed* notes, thus—*(Teacher,)* "O be joyful in the Lord," *(Leaders,)* "all ye lands;" *(Teacher,)* "serve the Lord with gladness, and

* The words have been arranged according to the rules contained in "The Instructions of Chenaniah," by the Rev. J. A. Latrobe, M. A.

come before his" *(Leaders)* "presence with a song." Let the same passage be repeated in a similar manner by the teacher and leaders, while at a signal the mass of the school join the leaders in the pronunciation of their portions. The chant may then be *sol-fa'd*. Afterwards the teacher and leaders may *sing* what they have been *saying*, the teacher singing the words belonging to the chanting note as a solo, (in the style of a recitative,) but pointing to the intervals on the Ladder as soon as the school ought to join her in singing the words which belong to the *timed* notes. When the pupils are sufficiently advanced, they will of course be directed to accompany the teacher in all the words of the chant; the teacher will then point at the same time to the *chanting* note, as well as the *timed* notes on the Musical Ladder.

XVII.

In a school where the cultivation of music was allowed to occupy so much time, that the voice would become wearied, if kept in constant exercise, the following varieties might perhaps be profitably introduced.

Let the tune be read in turn by the girls who compose each company, under the superintendence of their leaders.

Let small portions of a tune be sung in turn by the companies. Let the leaders set patterns, then rest while the majority are aided in their imitation by the instructress.

Let one half of the scholars beat time, while the other half sing, and *vice versa.*

Let the scholars write tunes from dictation on slates. Let them write the words of a psalm and insert the bars. Those who are more advanced, might transfer tunes from the old into the new, and from the new into the old notation. See Appendix, which contains rules for facilitating such an exercise. While the majority are employed in writing, one or two individuals might exercise themselves in playing on the Harmonicon.

XVIII.

TONE.

The scholars should be directed to hold themselves in an erect posture, to open their chests well, to separate the teeth enough to admit the thickness of the tips of two fingers, to extend the corners of the mouth far enough to prevent it from being round, to take care that nothing be heard of the nose, the teeth, or throat, but to send the breath freely and straight from the chest, with a direct aim at the note to be sounded. Some persons have a habit of sounding a lower note before they perform the proper note, and thus produce a very unpleasant clack, not unlike that heard in pumping, or the cry of a person driving cows; for example, if *Doh* were the intended note, they would preface it by a quick *Sole*, thus—

$$\left\{\begin{matrix}\text{how-oo} \\ \text{s} \quad \mathbf{D}\end{matrix}\right\}$$

But an exaggerated imitation of defects as they occur, is usually more intelligible to children than precepts, and the production of voice in any shape must be aimed at before refinement of manner. Sometimes interest in the art of singing may be increased, by a short explanation of the wonderful internal instrument by which they sing. Compare the lungs to the bellows of an organ—the chest to the box which contains them, and tell the children that instead of a row of pipes like an organ, one for each note, they have a pipe so curiously framed, that it is made to change its shape for every tone. Call their attention to the Maker and Giver of this instrument, and ask them, to what use they should delight to apply it? Ps. cxxxix. 14, "I will praise Thee, for I am fearfully and wonderfully made." Direct them to draw in plenty of breath, and to spend it judiciously. For this purpose, exercise them in holding a note as long as they can; tune may be cultivated at the same time by an accompaniment of other tones in the chord. In an early stage of singing, I think it better for pupils to *imitate the unvarying tone of an organ pipe, when no pedal is employed, than to attempt to swell and diminish the quantity of sound:* in swelling, beginners are apt to be too sharp, and in diminishing, too flat; besides which, pleased with the new acquirement, they will perhaps apply it to every long note, howl like gusts of wind, and injure tune, accent, and expression. Let the pupils be directed sometimes to sing a tune as loud as they can, then as soft as possible; afterwards, when acquired by heart, the quantity of tone may be regulated by signals according to the expression; at the same time, let not the accent be disregarded. In singing the common chord, (see Lesson V,) accustom the children to proportion the sounds equally; otherwise the upper *Doh* will probably be louder than the total sound of the other three intervals of the chord. Discretion however is requisite in enforcing this desirable softness in upper notes, lest pupils be discouraged; it is so much more difficult to produce high soft tones of good intonation than loud tones, that the latter should be secured first. If the common chord is thoroughly well executed, the effect resembles that of a musical glass, touched by a moistened finger, in circular motion. When singing a tune, the pupils should be cautioned against dividing a musical foot in taking breath; and when words are added, they must also avoid dividing a word. I believe most singers spend their breath too rapidly. It is desirable to draw it in freely and silently.

XIX.

EXPRESSION.

When skill in *Melody, Harmony, Rhythm,* and *Tone* has been acquired, the next thing to be considered is *Expression.* Before sacred words are attached to a tune, the expression should be regulated simply by the sentiment appertaining to the music. If the tune be worth anything, it will bear the character of plaintive or grave, or serene, or cheerful, or triumphant, or perhaps a mixed and varied expression may belong to it. The principal perfection of music consists in speaking a language more refined than words can convey; yet the expression here alluded to, should be subject to any variation of that which is dependent upon the words; of course a judicious instructor will select with care such a tune as will best correspond with the general sentiment of the poetry; and if the choir "sing" "with understanding," no caution need be given against a drawling manner when the strain should be cheerful, nor against sprightly turns and languishing slides, nor against a careless, boisterous, or jovial style on any occasion; nor, supposing all mechanical difficulty in singing surmounted, need any protest be entered against bawling, howling, crowing, or screaming; attention to what may be termed the *sentiment of the psalm tune* would, I conceive, check the attempts which some vocalists make to sing a tenor part an octave higher than the composer intended, and deter them from introducing notes at random above the tunes; a practice, which, if it became common in a congregation, would confuse the harmony, and drown the proper melody. Here I will venture to notice more particularly the "drawling" style above-mentioned. It prevailed and was lamented in the time of Dr. Watts. (See preface to Dr. Miller's Psalms, page ii.) And I conceive it will not be eradicated, where pauses are considered legitimate at the end of a line, before the conclusion of the tune and stanza.

I am aware this practice has the sanction of custom and high authority, but may it not have originated in the condescension of a leader to the infirmities of an uninstructed congregation, who are glad of these halts to take breath and of these hints by which they are aided in attaching words to a tune? The consequence of such condescension appears to me to be as follows. The regular return of the accent being interrupted before the conclusion of the tune, the congregation lose the sense of time; perhaps they employ part of the leader's pause in prolonging the last note of the line, then they listen for the leader to recommence; a complaisant leader, in return, listens to hear whether the congregation have joined him, before he proceeds to the next note, and a *drawling infection* spreads through the remaining notes. Even without these designed pauses, there is a tendency in a congregation, unprovided with notes, to *drawl*, because they are obliged to follow, rather than accompany their leader, when they do not know a tune by heart. Whatever conscientious objections may be advanced against Oratorios, is there any reason why a tune of the triumphant character of the 149th psalm, should not be sung with all the animation of such a passage as "Wake the lute and strike the lyre," in the second chorus in Athalia?

The directions respecting expression have been chiefly of a negative order, and it is difficult to give many precepts of a positive nature on the subject. Emphasis on a word of peculiar importance may sometimes be effected by a forcible (and perhaps abrupt) execution of it; but how can rules be defined for the expression, which should belong to strains of *lamentation, entreaty, tenderness, confidence, thankfulness, adoration, exultation?* The example of a judicious instructor may do much in leading a pupil to sing with expression, but feeling and good sense in the scholar will do more, when once attention is directed to the point. Singing is closely connected with recitation, and in both cases correct pronunciation is important. Glaring improprieties in this respect may be considerably counteracted in charity shools, by the adoption of the

"Pronouncing Spelling Lessons;"* and when ladies interest themselves in teaching poor children, their tuition has of course a tendency to check that vulgarity of manner, which, amongst other causes, has debased psalmody. Though some directions may be given for performing psalmody with judicious expression, yet of course it is neither by human rules nor example, that the devotional spirit with which psalms should be sung can be taught; but may we not hope, that if the altar be built, the wood laid in order, and the sacrifice prepared, respect may be had unto the offering, and fire be sent down, which will make prayer and praise ascend up as grateful incense? The true spirit in which psalms and hymns and spiritual songs should be sung, (Col. iii. 16.) ought ever to be kept in view by the instructor. When a tune has been well acquired in a school, with the *Sol-fa* letters, and sacred words are to be attached to it, let strict silence be required for a few moments, then let the children rise at a signal, without being heard, let the words be read seriously and impressively, and, perhaps,

* Price 7s. large type.

a few observations and questions interspersed to draw attention to the sense of them.

Decorum in the cultivation of psalmody, is surely not more requisite in children than in adults; and it would be very desirable that every choir should be under the direction of some one who would be watchful over this point. Another desideratum is, that when singing has formed a part of actual worship, caution be exercised respecting the making of it afterwards a subject of criticism; for although the congregation in general may reap some benefit from remarks made in private on the choir, yet may not the effect on the minds of the individuals who compose it be injurious? may they not be led to regard the church as a concert room, and seek to sing to their own "praise and glory?" A grand temptation to this evil will be removed, if psalmody be ever sufficiently cultivated, to render the execution of it easy and general; a congregation might then cease to be divided, as is too frequently the case, into performers and audience; and their mingled voices form one full ocean of harmony, representing the union and melody of heart which should characterize the assembly as members of one mystical body! May the great Head of it deign to accompany this little work with His blessing!

APPENDIX.

DIRECTIONS FOR TEACHING THE SYSTEM OF NOTATION BY POINTS, TO A CLASS OF SCHOLARS ALREADY ACQUAINTED WITH THE SOL-FA NOTATION, AND RULES FOR TRANSFERRING A TUNE FROM THE OLD INTO THE NEW CHARACTERS.

Let the instructer avoid applying the names A, B, C, &c. to the points of the old notation before the scholars are familiar with the use of the points as scale-notes.

I.

Exhibit to the class diagrams on a large scale, of the Stave, of the Table of Degrees and of Clefs.

STAVE.

TABLE OF DEGREES.

CLEFS.

Let the teacher be furnished with a key containing the following explanations and questions.

The instructer should point to the diagrams while describing them.

STAVE.

EXPLANATION.

Five lines drawn over each other form a Stave or Staff, viz. a support for the notes of music. *On* these lines and *in* the spaces between them, the heads of the notes are placed.

1st line, 2nd line, 3rd line, 4th line, 5th line.

5
4
3
2
1

1st space, 2nd space, 3rd space, 4th space.

4
3
2
1

QUESTIONS AND ANSWERS.

How many lines drawn over each other form a stave? *Five.*

How many spaces are there between the lines? *Four.*

Is the first line at the bottom or top of the stave? *At the bottom of the stave.*

Is the first space at the bottom or top of the stave? *At the bottom of it.*

Where are the heads of the notes placed? On *the lines and* IN *the spaces of the stave.*

TABLE OF DEGREES.

EXPLANATION.

The Table of Degrees is composed of two staves, and one line between them. The pitch of this line is always O, and the Table of Degrees forms a regular flight of steps for the notes of the *Doh* scale in O column.

QUESTIONS AND ANSWERS.

Of how many staves is the Table of Degrees composed? *Two.*

What is the pitch of the line between them? *O.*

[Let the pupils be exercised in reading the notes as scale-notes from the middle *Doh* upwards, and from the middle *Doh* downwards, and then dodge them in the following manner.]

What note stands on the first line of the upper stave? *Me.*

What note stands in the third space of the upper stave? *Doh.*

What note stands on the fifth line of the lower stave? *Lah.*

What note is in the space between the O line and the highest line of the lower stave? *Te.*

CLEFS.

EXPLANATION.

A Clef is a mark that shews which lines and spaces of this Table of Degrees are used for the stave. The four clefs most in use are Treble, Counter-Tenor, Tenor, and Bass.

QUESTIONS AND ANSWERS.

What is the design of a clef? *It shews which lines and spaces of the Table of Degrees are used for the stave.*

What are the names of the four clefs most in use? *Treble, Counter-Tenor, Tenor, and Bass.*

II.

TABLE OF KEYS.

A Table of Keys such as is found in the beginning of the "Guide to Sol-fa-ing," on a large scale, should be suspended before the pupils, the teacher should then say, pointing respectively to the various signs on it—

EXPLANATION.

The points in this Table are arranged in the same order as the scale-notes on the cylinder in the harmonicon. This row agrees with O column. The row above with W column; the row below with Y column. This sign ♯ is called a sharp; this ♭ a flat. When the clef is treble clef, (as you see it is on all these staves,) and there is no sharp or flat after it, the stave is like the upper stave in the Table of Degrees; the lower *Doh* therefore stands on the O line. Here is a short piece of the O line, on which stands the point, *Doh*—

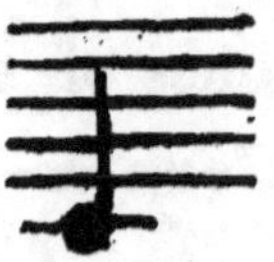

(observe that a short part of a line is called a ledger line.) *Te* stands on the space just below the O line; *Lah* stands on another ledger line, which is part of the highest line in the lower stave of the Table of Degrees, as you have been told before.

QUESTIONS AND ANSWERS.

In what order do the points in this table stand? *In the same as the scale-notes on the cylinder in the harmonicon.*

What is this sign? *A sharp.*

What is this? *A flat.*

What is this clef? *Treble clef.*

If no sharp or flat follows it, with what column does the stave agree? *O column.*

What is a ledger line? *A short part of a line.*

On what ledger line does *Doh* stand? *The middle O line.*

On what space does *Te* stand? *The space just below the O line.*

Does the ledger line on which the lowest *Lah* stands, belong to the higher or lower stave in the Table of Degrees? *The lower.*

EXPLANATION.

A clef with one or more sharps or flats after it is called the Signature. If there be sharps in the Signature, the last sharp stands on *Te;* if there be flats in the Signature, the last flat stands on *Fah.*

QUESTIONS AND ANSWERS.

What forms the signature? *A clef with one or more sharps or flats after it.*

On what space does the sharp stand in Y column? *The first.*

Then on what line does *Doh* stand? *The second line.*

In what space does the last sharp in Q column stand? *The third space.*

Then on what line does *Doh* stand? *The fourth line.*

On what line does the flat stand in W column? *The third.*

Then on what space does *Doh* stand? *The first.*

[The instructress may exercise the pupils in singing a tune, (with the time of which they are already acquainted,) while she points to the intervals on the Table of Keys, in the same manner as she would to those in the Musical Ladder, with this difference, that in the Table of Keys her hand must move horizontally as on the harmonicon, instead of perpendicularly as on the Ladder. The teacher should previously put queries of the following kind. If the tune be *Wakefield*, she will say—]

QUESTIONS AND ANSWERS.

There are three sharps, what is the column? *H.*

On what line does the last of the three sharps stand? *The second line.*

What scale-note is on the same line? *Te.*

Then in what space is *Doh?* *The second space.*

III.

TABLE OF TIME.

[This Diagram (found also in the "Guide to Sol-fa-ing," on a small scale,) may be suspended before the pupils, while the teacher explains it.]

EXPLANATION.

The signs and names of notes, according to the time they occupy, is as follows.

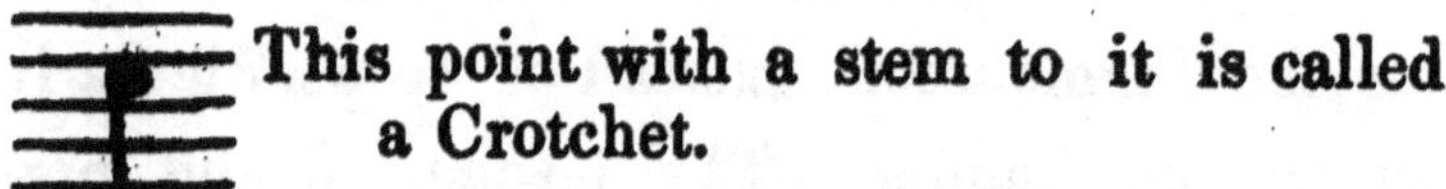
This point with a stem to it is called a Crotchet.

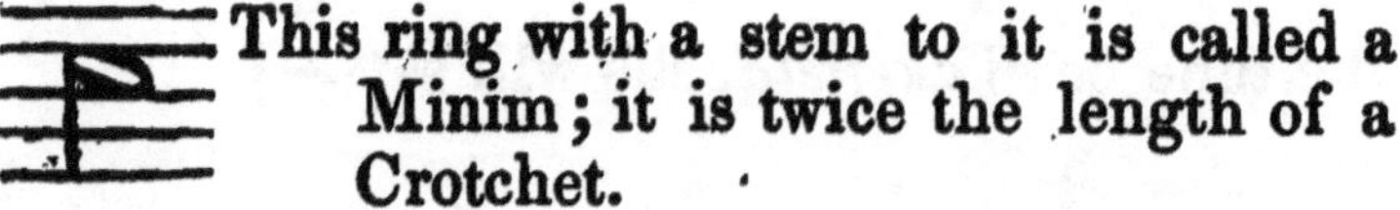
This ring with a stem to it is called a Minim; it is twice the length of a Crotchet.

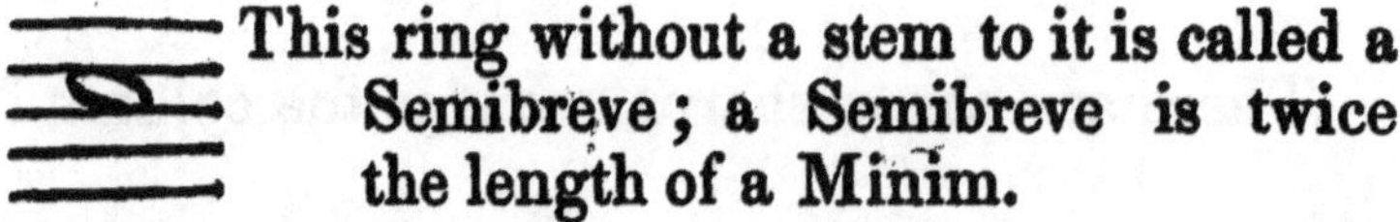
This ring without a stem to it is called a Semibreve; a Semibreve is twice the length of a Minim.

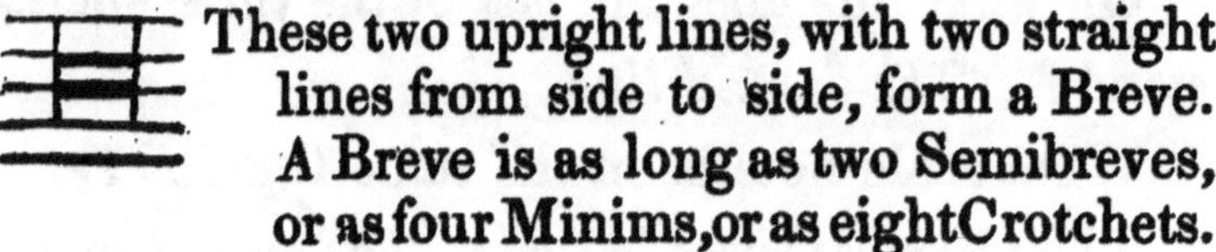
These two upright lines, with two straight lines from side to side, form a Breve. A Breve is as long as two Semibreves, or as four Minims, or as eight Crotchets.

QUESTIONS AND ANSWERS.

What is this? [pointing to the diagram.] *A Crotchet.*

If the scholar at the head of the class sings eight Crotchets, how many Minims might the second girl sing in the same time? *Four.*

How many Semibreves might the third girl sing in the same time? *Two.*

How many Breves might the fourth girl sing during the same time? *One only.*

EXPLANATION.

This point, with a stem and a hook to it, is called a Quaver; a Quaver is half the length of a Crotchet.

This point, with a stem and two hooks to it, is a Semiquaver.

This point, with a stem and three hooks to it, is a Demisemiquaver.

QUESTIONS AND ANSWERS.

What note is this? *A Quaver.*

How many Quavers may be sung in the time of one Crotchet? *Two.*

How many Semiquavers in the same time? *Four.*

How many Demisemiquavers in the same time? *Eight.*

EXPLANATION.

When notes, instead of being hooked, are joined together thus, they are said to be grouped.

A dot after a note, makes it half as long again as it would have been without it.

QUESTIONS AND ANSWERS.

When notes which, if single, would be hooked, are joined together thus, [pointing to an example in the Table of Time,] what are they said to be? *Grouped.*

How much does a dot prolong a note? *Half its own length.*

[The tune which had been sung while the instructress pointed to the Table of Keys, may then be read from a copy of a tune, in the usual notation by points, as it stands in the Guide to Sol-fa-ing. Should it be the *Wakefield,* let the *Sol-fa* letters be omitted except the first *Doh.* If the class be backward, let the pupils read only the *Sol-fa* letters, but when sufficiently advanced, let them read it thus, in portions—Doh minim—Me crotchet and quaver —Ra quaver—Sole minim—Fah minim—Me minim, &c. Then the tune may be sung.]

IV.

ACCIDENTALS.

EXPLANATION.

When a sharp or flat comes in any place except the signature, it is called an Accidental. A sharp raises a note half a tone, viz. makes it belong to one glass higher on the harmonicon; a flat lowers it half a tone. For example, a sharp placed before *Fah* in *O* column, raises it into the *Te* of *Y* column, [let this change be pointed out in the Table of Keys.] A flat, placed before *Te*, lowers it into the *Fah* of *W* column.

QUESTIONS AND ANSWERS.

If a sharp or flat occurs any where, except in the signature, what is it called? *An Accidental.*

Does a sharp raise or lower a note? *Raises it.*

What does a flat do? *Lowers it.*

If a sharp be placed before *Fah* in *O* column what change takes place? *Fah in O column is changed into the Te in Y column.*

If a flat is placed before *Te* in *O* column what change takes place? *Te in O column becomes Fah in W column.*

EXPLANATION.

An Accidental raises or lowers a note only through one measure, that is from one line called a bar, to the next bar; if the note is to be kept raised or lowered in another measure, the sharp or flat must be repeated.

QUESTION AND ANSWER.

How long does an accidental keep a note raised or lowered? *Through a measure; that is to say, from one bar to the next.*

EXPLANATION.

Besides a sharp and flat, there is another sign used for raising or lowering a note; it is called a natural, [point out an example in the Guide to Sol-fa-ing.] If the signature has flats in it the natural answers the purpose of a sharp, if the signature has sharps in it, the natural answers the purpose of a flat.

QUESTIONS AND ANSWERS.

If the signature has a flat in it, does a natural raise or lower a note? *Raises it.*

If the signature has a sharp in it, does a natural raise or lower a note? *Lowers it.*

[A tune with change of key may then be sung, while the instructress points to the intervals on the Table of Keys; it may then be read from a copy of the tune, and afterwards sung.

When the pupils practise a tune in which modulation occurs, let the letters necessary to express the change be inserted in the copy, and the remainder omitted except the first *Doh.*]

THE FOLLOWING DIRECTIONS ARE CALCULATED FOR THE INSTRUCTION OF INDIVIDUAL PUPILS, RATHER THAN OF A WHOLE CLASS.

The scholar may be exercised in transferring from the old into the new notation, tunes of various pitch, in which no change of column occurs. Then sing the tune from the *Sol-fa* letters, and afterwards from the points.

When facility in this exercise is acquired, the pupil may proceed to a tune in which modulation occurs.

The changes expressed by accidentals amongst the six related keys are as follows,—

♯ or ♮ before F makes it t See Mt. Ephraim.
♭ . ♮ . . T . . *f* Brunswick.
♯ . ♮ . . S . . N 149th Psalm
♯ . ♮ . . R . . n
♯ . ♮ . . D . . *n* 96th Psalm.

The above changes do not overpass the bounds of the Musical Ladder; more remote modulation may be traced on the Table of Tune. For example, sometimes a ♯ or ♮ before DOH renders it me, three columns to the right; thus converting the LAH of the original column into doh. I suppose that a ♯ before ME would render it ne, three columns to the right, and a ♯ before LAH would change LAH into ne two columns to the right; but if remote modulation be very transient or abstruse, it may be better to express it by chromatic intervals. See page 30.

In transferring a tune from the old notation into the new, it must be remembered, that the non-repetition of an accidental after a bar, restores a degree to its former position.

It must also be observed, that in the old notation, sharps, flats and naturals bear reference to the *original* column; (viz. the column in which the tune begins,) in expressing a change of column in the new notation and applying *u*, *i*, &c. reference must be had to the *last* column. A description of the following process for translating a tune, may facilitate the operation.

1st.—Write DOH under the first note to which this title belongs.

2nd.—If a change of column occurs, write under the first note which has an accidental sharp, or flat, or natural, the letter which *will* belong to it when the change of column is made.

3rd.—Select a note, on which express the change of column by adding *i* or *u*, *aw* or *oo*, &c. to the first *Sol-fa* letter, sung in the new column. In making this change, care should be taken that the first note in the new column be nearer than its octave to the last note in the preceding column.

4th.—Write the proper *Sol-fa* letter under the first note which occurs after it is restored to its original position, and then select a note, to be treated according to the preceding rule.

When the instructer has prepared a tune in the above manner, the pupil may write the intervening *Sol-fa* letters. It will be desirable to exercise the scholar in two or three examples in one rule before being introduced to another. When sufficiently advanced, scholars should express the change of column themselves.

They may also be exercised in transferring music from various clefs into the *Sol-fa* notation. In that case it may be well to remind them that by the signature it is easy to discover on what line or space DOH is placed, as—

the last sharp ♯ in it is on the degree on which stands *Te*. For example,

Column Y.

the last flat ♭ in the signature is on the degree on which stands *Fah*.

For example,

Column W.

N. B. If a scholar, acquainted with the *Sol-fa* notation, were to be taught to play a keyed instrument, a *Sol-fa* card, price 1s. for the piano-forte, might be of considerable assistance; I would also suggest the expediency of using a keyed *Sol-fa* harmonicon for the practice of exercises, as far as its limited compass will allow, instead of so expensive an instrument as a piano-forte. I beg leave also to point out the superiority of the former instrument to the latter, as an assistant to the vocal practitioner, on account of its freedom from fluctuation in tune.

I would likewise observe, that the small cylinder, containing the twelve major keys, with their relative minors arranged in the order in which modulation is most natural, initiates the practitioner insensibly into much of the theory of music. The portableness of this compact little instrument, which is less than two feet square, and one foot high, may also be reckoned among its recommendable qualities.

FINIS.

Printed by Jarrold and Sons, 3, London-Street, Norwich.

A Valentine sent to the Authoress.

Feby. 1841. —

The good people who live afar off in the moon
Are in want of some "Scheme" wh. their voices may tune
They have sent round to Saturn & Jupiter, Mars,
To Mercury, Venus, & e'en the fixed Stars,
But through comets & suns in their search they've combined
The Spirit of Harmony ne'er could they find:
In Saturn indeed they attempted to sing,
But the tenor & base being placed in the ring
The Harmony seemed as if to & fro toss'd
And the voices between in the chasm were lost.
The "fair maids of Venus too, they raised some strains,
But more on their looks than their sounds bestow'd pains:
The thunders in Jupiter awful arise,
And Mercury's wings beat the air as he flies;
Whilst in Mars nought is heard of harmonious sounds
But what from the clashing of armour resounds.
Yet still from the Earth when they listen at eve
Such sweet strains are wafted as seraphs might give
And they hear too 'tis this that inflames all their hearts
A "Magician" lives there who this knowledge imparts,
That all that she needs, is to flourish her wand
Straightway Men, Women, Children obey her command,
That all Animal nature is taught to Sol-fa
The cows to low "Moo" & the Sheep to bleat "Baa":
That Birds, "Bats" & Reptiles in glees are chiming,
That [illegible] "in trios"; & insects click time.

With as great a respect then as ever was paid
To the Emperor of China when the "Kow tow" is made;
They petition the Author of Sol-fa to send
Some teacher of Music instruction to lend;
And they trust that in time as the tones by [illegible]
Soft sounds may thence come through the [illegible]
Which may show that their teaching has [illegible]
But how anxious they've been due improvement [illegible]
And further they beg she will deign to partake
Of the offering they send, a lunar plum cake.
They hope that their packet may reach [illegible]
At the season that gave good St Valentine [illegible]
Because they have heard & believe it is true,
That free & full leave is then granted to do
What at some other time might a liberty seem,
But it - now (as it is) no presumption they deem.
And many a hearty & kind wish they send
That all good may the "Mighty Enchantress" attend.
And trusting she'll send them an answer right soon,
Subscribe themselves humbly

her friends in the moon.

Volcanic Valley
The Moon.

P.S. Passengers may be conveyed, or parcels, & letters forwarded by the Atmos-pheric Railroad.

By Miss Catherine Randall, Lower Clyde [illegible]

www.ingramcontent.com/pod-product-compliance
Lightning Source LLC
LaVergne TN
LVHW061219060426
835508LV00014B/1363

* 9 7 8 1 5 3 5 8 1 0 7 9 1 *